J 155.93 BOW
33292014003424
wpa
Bow, James, 1972-, author.
Dealing with loss

S0-AEQ-049

Wapiti regional library

Straight Talk About...
DEALING WITH LOSS

James Bow

Crabtree Publishing Company
www.crabtreebooks.com

Straight Talk About.

Produced for Crabtree Publishing by:
Infinch Solutions

Publishing Director: Ravi Lakhina

Author: James Bow

Project Controller: Vishal Obroi

Editors: John Perritano, Rebecca Sjonger

Proofreader: Shannon Welbourn

Art director: Dibakar Acharjee

Designer: Kabir

Project coordinator: Kelly Spence

Production coordinator: Margaret Amy Salter

Prepress technician: Margaret Amy Salter

Consultant: Jessica Alcock, Residential Counselor BA Psychology, MA Child and Youth Studies

Photographs:
Cover: CREATISTA / Thinkstock
Title page: MitarArt / Shutterstock Inc.; p.4: Paul Matthew Photography / Shutterstock Inc.; p.6: Paul Matthew Photography / Shutterstock Inc.; p.8: Kzenon / Shutterstock Inc.; p.9: cloki / Shutterstock Inc.; p.10: somchai rakin / Shutterstock Inc.; p.12: vita Lana K / Shutterstock Inc.; p.13: Ana Blazic Pavlovic / Shutterstock Inc.; p.14: Piotr Marcinski / Shutterstock Inc.; p.16: coloursinmylife / Shutterstock Inc.; p.18: Axente Vlad / Shutterstock Inc.; p.20: auremar / Shutterstock Inc.; p.21: Alexander Image / Shutterstock Inc.; p.22: Alexander Trinitatov / Shutterstock Inc.; p.26: bikeriderlondon / Shutterstock Inc.; p.28: DavidTB / Shutterstock Inc.; p.29: threerocksimages / Shutterstock Inc.; p.30: wavebreakmedia / Shutterstock Inc.; p.31: Dayna More / Shutterstock Inc.; p.32: Aleshyn_Andrei / Shutterstock Inc.; p.34: Odua Images / Shutterstock inc.; p.35: Monkey Business Images / Shutterstock Inc.; p.37: Diane Garcia / Shutterstock Inc.; p.38: Edyta Pawlowska / Shutterstock Inc.; p.40: Itsra Sanprasert / Shutterstock Inc.; p.41: YanLev / Shutterstock Inc.; p.42: Twin Design / Shutterstock Inc.

Library and Archives Canada Cataloguing in Publication

Bow, James, 1972-, author
        Dealing with loss / James Bow.

(Straight talk about...)
Includes index.
Issued also print and electronic formats.
ISBN 978-0-7787-2201-4 (bound).--ISBN 978-0-7787-2205-2 (pbk.).--ISBN 978-1-4271-9976-8 (pdf).--ISBN 978-1-4271-9972-0 (html)

        1. Loss (Psychology)--Juvenile literature. 2. Grief--Juvenile literature. I. Title. II. Series: Straight talk about...

BF575.D35B68 2015   j155.9'3   C2014-908097-2
                                                                    C2014-908098-0

Library of Congress Cataloging-in-Publication Data

Bow, James.
 Dealing with loss / James Bow.
     pages cm. -- (Straight talk about...)
   Includes index.
  ISBN 978-0-7787-2201-4 (reinforced library binding) -- ISBN 978-0-7787-2205-2 (pbk.) -- ISBN 978-1-4271-9976-8 (electronic pdf) -- ISBN 978-1-4271-9972-0 (electronic html)
 1. Loss (Psychology)--Juvenile literature. 2. Grief--Juvenile literature. 3. Death--Juvenile literature. I. Title.

BF575.D35B69 2015
155.9'3--dc23
                                    2014045075

Crabtree Publishing Company

www.crabtreebooks.com   1-800-387-7650

Printed in Canada / 022015 / MA20150101

Copyright © **2015 CRABTREE PUBLISHING COMPANY.** All rights reserved. No part of this publication may be reproduced, stored in a retrieval system or be transmitted in any form or by any means, electronic, mechanical, photocopying, recording, or otherwise, without the prior written permission of Crabtree Publishing Company. In Canada: We acknowledge the financial support of the Government of Canada through the Canada Book Fund for our publishing activities.

Published in Canada
Crabtree Publishing
616 Welland Ave.
St. Catharines, ON
L2M 5V6

Published in the United States
Crabtree Publishing
PMB 59051
350 Fifth Avenue, 59th Floor
New York, NY 10118

Published in the United Kingdom
Crabtree Publishing
Maritime House
Basin Road North, Hove
BN41 1WR

Published in Australia
Crabtree Publishing
3 Charles Street
Coburg North
VIC, 3058

CONTENTS

Meredith stares at the blood on her wrist.

It's been six months since her boyfriend died in a car accident. She went to the wake and then the funeral. At first, friends and family members said how sorry they were that Jake had died. People told her how strong she was because they didn't see her cry.

Meredith hasn't cried all that much in the months since Jake's death. Instead, she's felt numb and alone. Over time, people stopped talking about her boyfriend. Although she doesn't say anything, it hurts. How can they move on when she hasn't? Or can't?

She feels as bad as she felt six months ago. It's like every other emotion in her has been removed. She can't feel anything else, and a part of her wants that to change. That's why she took a knife and started cutting into her arm, bleeding into the bathroom sink. She needed to feel something, even pain.

She knows this isn't normal. Something is wrong. She shouldn't be feeling this way. She needs help.

Meredith picks up the phone and calls a helpline.

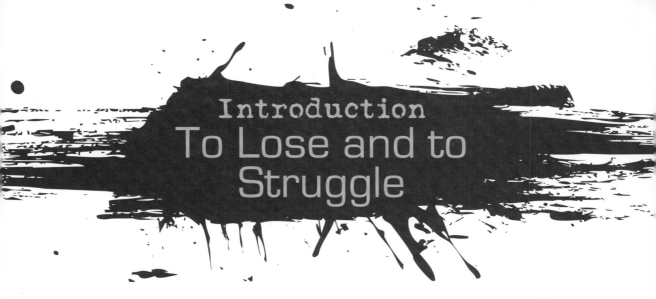

Introduction
To Lose and to Struggle

Six months ago, Meredith received a terrible shock. The sudden and unexpected death of her boyfriend was a blow. What followed, though, was common for someone struggling to deal with a loss.

Like Meredith, many teenagers grieve for lost loved ones, or are dealing with other traumatic events, such as the end of a relationship or a parent's divorce. Grief is what the mind does to heal itself. It's hard and it hurts, and only time can make the pain go away.

Unfortunately, in Meredith's case the pain didn't go away. It hurt so much and for so long that her grief turned to despair. Each year, thousands of teens in Meredith's situation intentionally injure themselves or think about suicide. That's when grief goes too far. Every day, doctors, psychiatrists, and therapists help kids and teenagers deal with their grief.

Meredith is lucky. She realized she needed help. She still has a long road ahead of her to deal with the pain, but she's taken the first step of the journey.

"I hate it when people think I should be grieving according to the 'stages' described in some high school health book. Since my sister's death I've learned that grief isn't five simple stages."
Kimberly, aged 17.

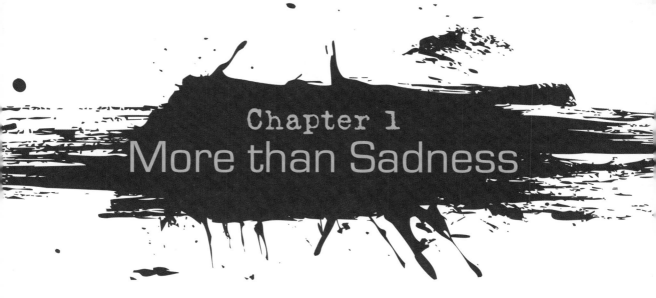

Chapter 1
More than Sadness

Losing things important to you is an unhappy part of life. Relationships end. Accidents happen. People get sick. Pets, friends, and loved ones all pass away. Grief is our natural response.

When you experience a loss, you feel sad. But grief is more than sadness. You may also feel angry because something important to you was taken away. You might feel overwhelmed. All of these feelings are normal. Grief is a natural reaction to any major change that seriously disrupts your life.

Grief is also unique. Every person deals with loss differently. There is no right or wrong way to feel. The process of grieving has no time limit.

Grief affects your mind and body in different ways. It can lead to mental and physical changes that, if you are not careful, can be harmful.

What Causes Grief?

Grief is how your brain reacts to major life changes, such as the death of a friend or a loved one. However, other things might cause you to grieve as well. These can include breaking up with a boyfriend or a girlfriend; the death of a pet; the divorce of your parents; moving to a new town; going to a different school; or ending a friendship.

Sudden change affects how we grieve. The death of a loved one after a long illness affects us differently than if that person were to die suddenly and unexpectedly. Sudden losses can be more difficult to deal with, but not always.

People grieve differently depending on the circumstances.

By the Numbers

- 1.2 million children currently in the United States will lose a parent by the age of 15.
- After losing a parent, 85 percent of American children experience **symptoms** such as difficulty sleeping, anger, worry, and **depression**.

Source: Dr. Elizabeth Weller, Director Ohio State University Hospitals

Samantha's Loss

Samantha lost her dad when she was 13. She knew all about grief because her grandmother had died the year before. This was different, though. "I didn't cry. I just stopped sleeping," she says. "I had to force myself out of bed each morning. People thought I was doing okay. I put on a fake smile and went to school as if everything was fine. It wasn't. On the inside, things that I enjoyed doing were now chores that took all my energy to do."

Some people just feel "numb" when a loved one dies.

From denial to acceptance, more or less, everyone goes through the same stages of grief.

Stages of Grief

Although each person grieves in his or her own way, most grief follows the same five stages. These stages of grief were first described by American psychiatrist Elisabeth Kübler-Ross in her 1969 book *On Death and Dying*. According to Kübler-Ross, the stages of grief are:

- *Denial and isolation:* When **trauma** hits, your mind can't process that the event is happening. You feel numb and you sometimes block out reality. This natural **defense mechanism** shields your mind from the shock.
- *Anger:* Once you get over the shock, anger sets in. You can direct the anger at the world, or at a higher power such as God, if you believe in one. Sometimes you might punch a wall, or you might unleash your anger at family, friends, or strangers. Anger is natural as you come to terms with the shock.
- *Bargaining:* Once you understand the trauma, your mind will look for some way to get rid of it, or blame something

or someone else for it. People often try to make a deal with a higher power. On the other hand, you may think you could have prevented this from happening. Feeling guilty is another part of the **bargaining** stage. You may say to yourself, "If only I'd seen the warning signs," or "If only I'd acted sooner." You can never bargain away what happened. You can't change the past.

- *Depression:* Depression, or sadness and regret, is the stage when you begin to understand what has happened. At this point, you worry about what the loss means and begin to regret things you've done or not done. You may also spend much of your time crying or feeling angry. You might disconnect from the things you love, possibly to avoid further loss.
- *Acceptance:* This is the final stage of grief. Your mind has processed what happened and is able to accept the trauma. You begin to "move on" with your life. This isn't to say that the grief goes away. For many people, grief never ends. Gradually, you remember the good times rather than the shock of the trauma. Not everybody is able to reach the acceptance stage, however.

The five stages of grief are not a road map, but a general path. Everybody copes in his or her own way. Some people go through two stages at once, or they slip back into a stage after moving out of it.

Laughter in Tears

You may have noticed that laughing and crying feel very similar. Some people switch from laughing to crying and back in an instant. Your body uses many of the same muscles to laugh as it does to cry. Both are powerful relievers of **stress** and emotion. If you find yourself laughing during sad times, don't worry—it's normal.

The Symptoms of Grief

People might say that grief is all in the mind. They're not wrong. However, grief can also lead to a number of changes that affect the body. Mental and physical symptoms include:

- *Strong emotions:* People expect you to be sad. They may even understand if you are angry. However, your mind is working overtime to deal with the trauma. As a result, emotions can be more intense. It might seem unusual to laugh at such a sad time, but it happens. It's not that you aren't grieving. The strong emotions released during the grieving process can be hard to contain and may come out in ways you don't expect.

- *Changes in appetite:* Have you ever been so upset that you don't feel hungry? That happens a lot when you're grieving. Other people who are grieving turn to food as a way to stop the pain. How often have you had ice cream, cookies, or chocolate when you felt upset?

- *Changes in sleep patterns:* Your mind is working so hard when you're grieving that it may be impossible to sleep. Other times, grief can be so exhausting that you feel like you want to sleep all the time.

- *Upset stomach:* Some people say grief can hit you "in the gut." It's true. Your body is reacting to stress. Your muscles ache from tension, including your stomach muscles. Stress also messes with your **immune system**, which makes it easier for you to get sick.

Your body can react physically to a loss.

- *Trouble concentrating:* It's sometimes hard to focus on things other than your grief, such as schoolwork, keeping appointments, and spending time with friends.
- *Low energy:* You can feel tired and **lethargic**. You're not sleeping. Your muscles are tense. That's because your mind is too busy dealing with the trauma. You don't think about other things. As a result, you don't have much strength or energy.

It is hard to concentrate when you're thinking about a trauma.

- *High blood pressure:* Grief is a form of stress. Stress can impact your body in a number of ways, including producing higher blood pressure, headaches, and muscle pain. In very serious cases, breathing can be difficult. You might experience chest pains. These serious symptoms should be reported to a doctor.

All of these symptoms are normal. They could happen to anyone dealing with a loss. The important thing is that you understand what is happening. Don't let these symptoms run your life or control your health.

By the Numbers

According to one survey of 531 children and teenagers who were grieving the loss of a parent or sibling, 46 percent said they couldn't believe their loved one had died. Moreover:
- 75 percent said they were feeling sad.
- 86 percent said that they wish they had more time with their loved one.
- 69 percent said they wish they could talk just once more to their loved one.
- 45 percent said they were having trouble concentrating on schoolwork.
- 34 percent said they said hurtful things to others.
- 73 percent think about their loved one every day.

Source: National Alliance for Grieving Children

"My friend went crazy into drugs, sex, and skipping school after her boyfriend got killed in a skiing accident. She stopped talking about him. Now she's kicked out of school and is pregnant by a guy she hates. Since my boyfriend's car accident, I know what can happen if I make wrong choices like her." Sara, aged 18.

Chapter 2
Dealing with Grief

Grief is a natural response to dealing with a loss. There's no avoiding it. You can't bring back relationships that have ended, and you can't bring the dead back to life. Only time can make the pain of grief feel less intense. This is difficult for someone who is grieving to hear. Grief is painful and hard to cope with.

Kids and teenagers may have a harder time dealing with grief than older people. Being a teenager is stressful enough. Your mind and your body are changing. You worry about how well you're doing at school, whether people like you, and what you want to do with your life. Add death or other trauma to the mix and it can all become overwhelming.

Not only that, kids and teens don't have as much experience in dealing with grief as older people do.

When Grief Becomes a Problem

Grief becomes a problem if it leads people to make decisions they wouldn't normally make, or if they hurt themselves. Grief can be so painful that we're tempted to try things to distract us from that pain.

Some people turn to drugs and alcohol as a way to make grieving seem less intense. Drugs and alcohol are not the answer. Not only do they cause health problems and cloud your thinking, they mask the pain for only a short while. Drugs and alcohol don't take away the pain.

Doctors can give you prescription drugs if you are having serious health issues while dealing with your loss, such as being unable to sleep or feeling depressed. Doctors know when to give the proper medicine, and how much you should take. They know the risks and how to keep you safe. You should never self-medicate.

Some people turn to drugs and alcohol when grief becomes overwhelming.

Shutting Down and Shutting Out

One of the hardest things about dealing with grief can be feeling as if you have to go through it alone. Grief is a personal experience. Most people will not understand what you are going through. After all, it's not their relationship that ended or their parent who passed away. They may find it hard to understand how you feel, and sometimes that can make people uncomfortable.

People who do understand may have their own grief to deal with. Grieving can impact your life in many ways. Activities such as going to school, playing sports, or hanging out with friends may seem less important to you.

It's one thing to take time to cope with your feelings and give yourself a chance to heal. However, withdrawing and doing nothing for too long can hurt you in many ways.

If you don't eat, you can become sick. If you skip school, you can make it harder to get into college. When grief leads you into depression, it can keep you from taking care of yourself. It can be hard to break out of the cycle.

On the Rebound

Grief can also cause some people to make bad decisions with relationships, even turning to risky behavior as a way to cope. You may have heard the phrase of two people getting together "on the rebound" of a breakup. The ending of a relationship can be a grief-filled time. Fears about being alone can cause some people to commit to a new relationship that they might later regret.

Friends might not seem so important when you're grieving.

Don't go at it alone when grieving.
There are people who can help.

When You Should Get Help

Although it might not seem like it at the time, grieving helps you feel better. However, if more than four months have passed and you don't feel any better, you might have a larger problem. If grief prevents you from taking care of yourself, including eating right or sleeping properly, then you may need help. Talk to an adult, or a counselor or doctor. They can get you the help you need to deal with your grief.

It's Okay to Cry—or Not Cry

You may find it difficult or embarrassing to cry. Crying can make some people uncomfortable. Crying, however, is a natural way to deal with grief. Crying releases the pain you're feeling. This helps your mind heal. If you want to cry, but don't feel comfortable doing it in front of others, you can find places or do things that make it a bit easier. For instance:

• Go for a walk and find a safe place where you can be by yourself to cry.

• Take a long, hot shower. Not only is it private, the water will muffle the sound of your tears.

• Rent tearjerker movies. These can be your "permission" to cry.

It's also okay not to cry. Some people may be expecting you to show stronger emotions when grieving, but you don't have to live up to their expectations. It's okay if you don't feel like crying.

Crying is healthy when you're grieving.

Grief can be so painful that it might seem as if things will never get better. This can lead to self-destructive behavior, such as self-cutting or thoughts of suicide. If this is happening to you or someone you know, pick up the phone and call a helpline right away. You can find the numbers to call on page 46 of this book. Chapter 3 deals with ways to seek support from others to help you handle your grief, and chapter 4 shows how you can help with a friend's grief.

By the Numbers

In one survey in the United States, kids and teens under the age of 18 who had lost a family member were asked about their family and home life after the loss.

- 71 percent said the adults in their lives supported them
- 43 percent said the adults spent more time with them after their loved one passed
- 33 said their guardian found it hard to "talk about personal stuff"
- 52 percent said talking about the death of their loved one with a friend was hard

Source: National Alliance for Grieving Children

Myths and Facts of Dealing with a Loss

Myth: The best thing we can do for a grieving friend is not to talk about their loss.

Fact: It can be uncomfortable to talk about the focus of someone's grief. We may think that talking about it will hurt that person. We're tempted to change the subject or avoid it altogether. This can make people who are grieving feel as though their loss is a burden they have to carry on their own.

For many people who are grieving, talking about their loss helps them deal with their pain. A shared burden is easier to carry. Yes, everybody grieves in his or her own way, and the person grieving may not want to talk about the loss. However, avoiding the subject can make their loss feel worse.

Myth: It's been months since the loss. Shouldn't the grieving person be over it by now?

Fact: Grief is a deep wound that can take a long time to heal. That process is different for every person. Research at Southern Illinois University School of Medicine suggests that an average person takes 18 months to two years to recover fully from grief. Some recover quickly, whereas others take much longer.

Myth: Saying the loss was "the will of God" or "they're in a better place now" comforts someone who is grieving.

Fact: Dorothy, quoted on the National Funeral Directors Association website (www.nfda.org), responds to this myth: "I was nine years old when my mother died and I was very sad. I did not join in the prayers at my parochial school [a school run by a religious organization]. Noticing that I was not participating, the teacher called me aside and asked what was wrong. I told her my mother died and I missed her, to which she replied, 'It was the will of God. God needs your mother in heaven.' But I felt I needed my mother far more than God needed her. I was angry at God for years because I felt he took her from me."

Myth: Crying a lot means you're going to have a nervous breakdown.

Fact: Crying is one way the brain deals with emotional trauma. Crying releases tension. Tears even wash away **toxins** the body produces. Not crying, if one feels the need to cry, can damage a person's mind and body, by bottling up strong emotions. Those pent-up feelings can stress out your body and mind.

"Right after my dad died, I felt like I needed to be strong for my mom. The only time I let myself cry was alone, in the dark of night. This holding in of my grief made it difficult for me to concentrate on anything but his death. Also, I didn't talk to people who would have listened to me, like my best friends, because I was jealous that they still had their dads and I didn't want to make them sad." Karen, aged 13.

Chapter 3
Family, Friends, and Grief

Sometimes when dealing with a loss, your friends and family aren't able to help you. They may be going through their own grief, or they might not understand how you feel. They know that you're in pain, but they don't know what to do about it.

As a result, people might say and do things that are meant to be helpful, but are actually hurtful. They may try to **rationalize** a loss by saying things such as the person is "in a better place" or the loss was part of a greater plan. They may try to fix the loss. In the case of a breakup, friends may set you up on dates. Parents may buy you a new pet to replace one that has passed away.

Get over It

Friends and family might ask, "Aren't you over it yet? It happened so long ago." They don't understand that it takes time to deal with a loss. If you're not ready, being pushed to get over your grief can be frustrating.

Worst of all, people might avoid talking about your loss, fearing they might upset you. It's okay if you don't feel like talking, but silence can make you feel alone. Some people might pull away from you.

Unfortunately, there is no easy way to deal with these problems. You can tell people that you want to talk about your loss. Your best friends will be there to listen to you. You may need to reach out to them, though.

Sometimes a hug from a friend says more than words.

The death of a family member is upsetting for everyone, especially a surviving spouse.

Shared Grief

If someone who is grieving has lost a parent, then the other parent is often grieving, too. That parent might be less responsive to the needs of a child. Grief affects parents just as it affects kids.

Adults dealing with losses go through the same stages of grief and experience many of the same problems as children. Grieving parents can lash out at their children. They may also become unresponsive, forgetting even to feed their kids. If that is the case, you need to turn to others for help.

Grief is a burden that you don't have to carry alone. If certain friends are uncomfortable with your grief, find other people who understand what you are going through and are willing to listen to you. If a parent isn't able to support you in your grief, perhaps another adult family member can help.

Finding Support

It can be hard to find supportive friends and family members. If you are having trouble, remember you're not alone. Millions of people deal with grief every day, and they know how hard it can be. They also know how alone it can make someone feel.

Many organizations have set up helplines that you can call to get help. There are also support groups you can join to share what you are experiencing with other people. Sometimes it's easier to talk to a stranger than to a friend or a family member. It's even easier if that person listens and understands. They know how you feel because they've felt a similar loss themselves.

There are also ways that you can help yourself cope. Some of these strategies are outlined in chapter 5. If you know someone who is grieving and you want to help, chapter 4 discusses some things you can do to support them.

Support groups can help you cope with your loss.

Connecting with an Adult

It's not unusual for kids and teenagers to feel alone during their most sorrowful times. One third of American children who lost a parent said in a survey that their current guardian found it hard to talk to them, while more than half said they wanted an adult to spend more time with them. However, the majority had an adult that gave these kids the support they needed.

The majority of kids and teens have a supportive adult to help them deal with a loss.

By the Numbers

When researchers asked kids and teenagers what the most helpful thing they did to deal with a loss was, this is what they said:
- Spend time with friends: 59 percent
- Listen to music: 49 percent
- Keep busy; do things: 46 percent
- Go to a grief group: 42 percent
- Talk to others who went through the same thing: 41 percent

Source: National Alliance for Grieving Children

"When my friend died, the rest of the world kept going and no one knew what I was going through. No one could understand the pain I was feeling. I wanted the world to stop and I wanted to just scream out, 'Doesn't anyone realize that I am hurt?' I kept looking at people and thinking, 'You don't have a care, and look at me, one of my friends just died.'" Amy, aged 16.

Chapter 4
Dealing with a Friend's Grief

Most of this book covers how kids and teenagers deal with their own grief. In the last chapter, we talked about getting support from friends and family. This chapter looks at how you can be a supportive friend to someone dealing with a loss.

A person's grief affects more than just the individual. It can also impact friends and close family members who want to help, but just don't know what to do. People who want to help a grieving friend can make the loss easier to bear. Friends can also see when grief is becoming a problem.

Don't Fix Everything

The best thing you can do to help is simply be there for your friend. Don't ignore someone's grief. If you're worried that bringing up the subject will make your friend sad, just be honest. Allowing your friend to talk about his or her loss will help.

It might be awkward at first, but just being there during your friend's time of grief can help a lot.

Don't try to fix your friend's grief. Avoid saying things such as, "It's all for the best," or "You'll get over it." Instead, say more helpful things like: "I'm sorry for what happened," or "I wish I had the right words, but know that I care." Talk about good memories you have of your friend's loved one, or ask questions about that person's life. Do not avoid saying his or her name—it's good to say it out loud.

Remember, you might see your friend get angry. He or she might even direct that anger at you. Don't take it personally. It's not about you; it's about your friend's loss. Don't shout back. Say again that you are there for him or her. Step back for a while until your friend calms down.

Admit that you can't make it better, and don't try to change your friend's feelings. Go out and do things together, such as getting a pizza. This will make sure he or she eats something. It will help your friend not pull away from the world around him or her.

Warning Signs

Spending time with your friend not only helps him or her deal with the loss, it gives you time to watch and make sure he or she is not having trouble dealing with the grief.

Keep an eye on your friend's weight, watching to see if it changes quickly. Look to see if his or her schoolwork is suffering. If you see cuts, bandages, or recent scars, these may be signs that your friend is cutting himself or herself in an attempt to deal with their emotional pain.

Friends are there for you during good times and bad.

Say What?

All of us can become tongue-tied when confronted with a friend's loss and not know what to say. Here are some helpful hints:

- Don't say: "I know how you feel."

- Say: "I can't imagine what you're going through."

- Don't say: "He's in a better place."

- Say: "I'm sorry for your loss."

- Don't say: "There's a reason for everything."

- Say: "You're in my thoughts and prayers."

- Don't say: "Be strong."

- Say: "I'm here for you."

Sometimes it's best not to say anything. Just be with the person. Give him or her a hug.

If your friend starts talking about hurting himself or herself, death, or suicide, talk to an adult you trust right away. Don't be afraid to call a therapist, a grief counselor, or a helpline if you're worried about the mental health of your friend. It's better to be safe than sorry.

Grief Revisited

Even when grief fades, it can come back. Many things can remind a person of what was lost. All it takes is a song, a familiar smell, or seeing something to bring back memories. When this happens, grief can come roaring back and become nearly overwhelming. Let your friend know that it is normal to react and cry.

Moving on doesn't mean forgetting.

"I Miss Sophie"

Sophie was Karen's dog, a chocolate lab with deep brown fur and eyes like marbles. Karen liked to say that Sophie had a "chocolate kiss nose." She lived a long time. It was a good life. Even so, Karen was devastated when Sophie suddenly died. "For a while, I couldn't even look at another dog without thinking of Sophie. I didn't get another dog for a long time. Then one day I went to the shelter, just to look. I still miss Sophie, but my new dog Loretta is cool, too."

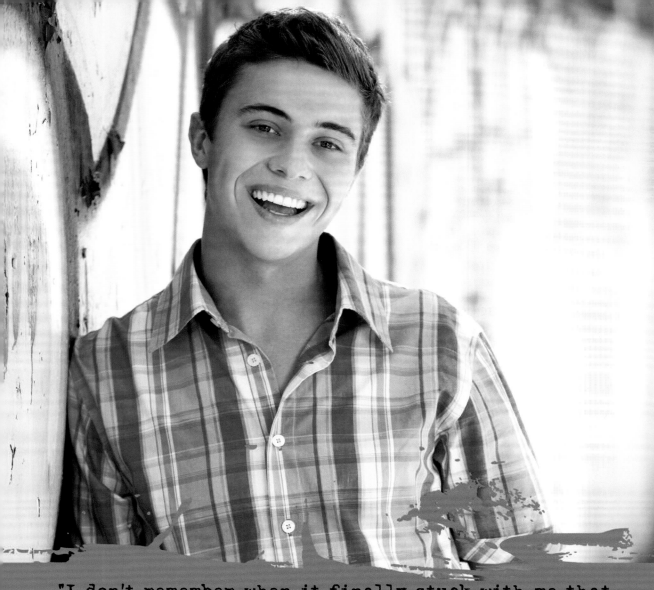

"I don't remember when it finally stuck with me that my dad was never coming back. I couldn't tell you when I was able to start talking about him again. I wish I could tell you that there's a magic day you can look forward to when things will be easier, but I can't. It just happened over time. The more I talked about things, the easier it got for me, and now I am able to remember and talk about my dad and smile." Sam, aged 17.

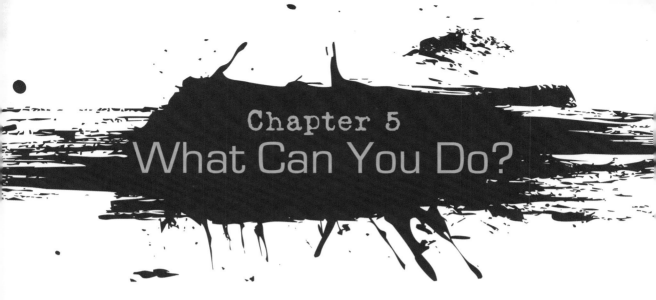

Chapter 5
What Can You Do?

Grief is manageable. The pain you feel over a breakup, the loss of a pet, or moving away from your friends will eventually fade. The death of a loved one is harder to overcome, but over time, your mind comes to terms with the loss rather than reliving it.

Don't avoid your grief, and don't deal with it on your own. Find people who will support you and find the strength to keep going. It can be done, and this chapter talks about what you can do to help yourself cope.

A Sample Grief Letter

Dear Angela:

We passed the second anniversary of your death earlier this week. It kind of snuck up on me. I wasn't thinking of the date until I spotted a calendar and it all clicked. Suddenly, the memories came flooding back. I felt ashamed of myself that I hadn't been thinking about you. I cried for a long time. Afterward, I felt better. Then I felt a little guilty again, but I know you'd want me to feel better.

Things are going okay here. The new semester starts next week. I have my classes picked out. My friends and I went to this assembly that was so boring you would have hated it. Let me tell you about Mr. Cheever and Ms. Reynolds...

How to Help Yourself

Talking to yourself is always a good idea if there's no one else you can turn to. It's a good way to help your mind work through your loss. You can write a letter to yourself or to the loved one you are missing. You could also write notes in a journal. You do not need to share your letter or journal with anyone. These can be private **outlets** for your feelings.

Writing is a good way to express your emotions.

Over time, you'll start doing the
things you normally would do.

The key to dealing with a loss is not to shut down.
We've described some of the physical symptoms you
can experience, such as changing sleep patterns and
lack of appetite. These things, while normal, can hurt
you if they go on for too long.

How can you get your body back into a regular
routine? Get out of the house and exercise. Try to eat,
even if you're not hungry. Go to bed when you usually
do, and don't sleep in longer than you usually do. Your
body needs its strength to help your mind deal with all
of the feelings surrounding your loss.

Bringing Closure

Grief is unique to each person. No one experiences it in
the same way. Coping is also unique. Still, there are a
number of things that can help people deal with grief.

Visiting the grave of a loved one can help bring closure.

For one thing, rituals, such as funerals, wakes, and memorial services, can help bring a sense of comfort and closure. Wakes, where people gather to remember the person who passed away, can soothe the pain of the loss. This is a good time to express your feelings and not keep them bottled up.

You can also join support groups set up by people who have gone through similar losses. People in support groups may better understand some of the emotions you're feeling, and they know how important it is to listen to you if you need to talk. Call one of the helplines or visit the online resources listed on page 46 of this book. They can point you to a group near where you live.

Visiting the grave site is also important. Sometimes it's a good idea to talk to the person you lost as if he or she is still alive. Explain how his or her death has affected you. Tell your loved one how you miss and loved him or her.

The Long Road

One of the worst parts of grief is the sense of aloneness. However, remember you are not alone. There are people you can turn to. Or a grieving friend may need to turn to you.

Grief changes in intensity and character over time. You will always miss the ones you love. After a while, you will focus more on the good memories from before your loss, rather than the trauma of the loss itself.

By the Numbers

One survey in the United States asked kids and teens who had suffered a loss how they remembered or honored the memory of what or who they had lost.

- 71 percent kept photos or special things that belonged to the person who died
- 65 percent had fun and enjoyed life
- 54 percent did things the person who died liked to do
- 53 percent told stories about the good times they'd had with their friend or family member

Source: National Alliance for Grieving Children

43

Hot Topics
Q&A

It's been months since my loss and my friends are telling me to get over it. Should I be getting over it?

A: You need to talk to friends who don't expect you to follow a set schedule for grieving. You're the one who is dealing with the grief, not your friends. They don't know how you feel. Everybody deals with grief in his or her own way. Sometimes it can take up to two years to deal fully with the trauma. You can let friends know that telling you to "get over it" is not okay. Find people who will listen to you without judging you, and talk to them about your feelings.

I feel just as terrible as I did when I first heard the news four months ago. I want this pain to end, and I don't see a way out of it. What can I do?

A: Even though we said you don't have to follow a timetable when it comes to your grief, if you ever feel that you are not getting better, or if you feel you can't cope with your grief, ask for help. Talk to someone you trust. If no one is available, call one of the help lines in this book.

I haven't cried since my dad died. Instead, I'm angry all the time. Is this normal?

A: Yes. Many people feel angry when someone dies. The death of someone close to you is a shock that produces many strong feelings, including anger. It's fine to be angry at the loss.

Understanding what the anger is truly about is helpful. Let it out in ways that won't hurt you or people around you. If you can't control your anger, talk to someone you trust, or talk to your doctor, a counselor, or call a helpline.

I had a huge fight with my best friend the day that he died. I know it wasn't my fault, but I still feel so guilty. How can I deal with that?

A: After someone dies, it's natural to regret the things you said or haven't said to him or her. That doesn't make the regret any less painful. One way you can cope with the guilt is writing your thoughts and feelings. Writing a letter to your best friend, even though he'll never receive it, will help you deal with your feelings. It also helps to talk about your regrets with someone you trust.

Other Resources

The following websites and helplines will provide you with trustworthy information about dealing with loss.

TeensHealth

http://kidshealth.org/teen/your_mind/emotions/someone_died.html
This helpful web page provides an overview on grief and the grieving process. It also includes information on grieving rituals, as well as stories and a Q&A section on dealing with loss. The information on the site is reviewed by medical experts to ensure everything is accurate and up-to-date.

The Dougy Center

www.dougy.org/grief-resources/how-to-help-a-grieving-teen
The website run by the National Center for Grieving Children & Families has many helpful resources, including a page dedicated to assisting grieving teens.

In the United States

Crisis Call Center

crisiscallcenter.org
1-800-273-8255
A 24-hour helpline and website providing safe, confidential, and non-judgmental help to anybody in any type of crisis, free of charge.

Teen Line

www.teenlineonline.org

(310) 855-HOPE

Text "TEEN" to 839863

A crisis helpline operated by teens, including a phone line operating from 6 p.m. to 10 p.m., Pacific Standard Time. The Web site also includes a message board where you can ask teens questions about whatever you are concerned about.

Trevor Project

www.thetrevorproject.org

1-866-4-U-TREVOR (1-866-488-7386)

If you are considering suicide or need help, call the 24-hour Trevor Project now.

In Canada

Kids Help Phone

www.kidshelpphone.ca

1-800-668-6868

Kids Help Phone is a Canadian crisis helpline for boys and girls, operated 24 hours a day, 365 days a year. Calls are confidential. Trained professionals offer counseling on many subjects, including abuse, drug and alcohol issues, parenting problems, school problems, and suicide prevention.

Glossary

bargaining Offering something to get something else back

defense mechanism Something your mind or body does to protect itself from shock or trauma

denial Not being able to believe or accept that something has happened

depression A mental illness that causes a person to feel extremely sad, angry, or frustrated for long periods of time

immune system Parts inside the body that fight off disease and infections

lethargic Feeling tired, slow, and not wanting to go anywhere or do anything

psychiatrist A doctor who deals with mental health issues

outlets Ways to release or satisfy an emotion or impulse

rationalize To explain or justify why something has happened

stress When things make you uncomfortable or upset for long periods of time

symptom A sign that something is wrong with your body or your mind

therapist A person who helps others deal with their mental health problems

toxins Chemicals that can be absorbed by or made by the body that hurt it

trauma A very upsetting, shocking, or painful experience

Index